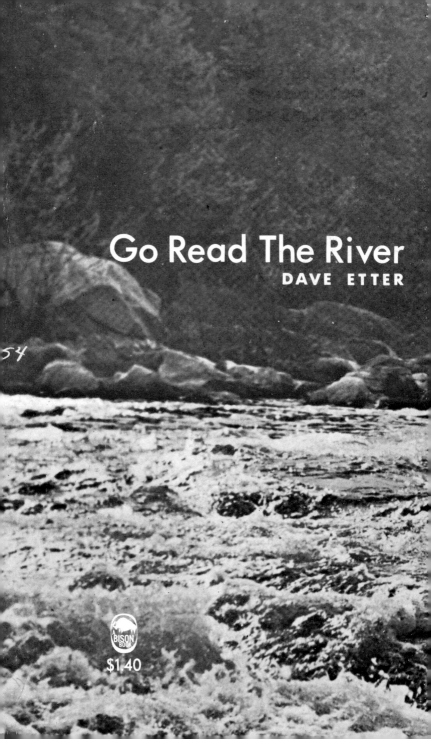

Go Read The River

DAVE ETTER

54

$1.40

GO READ THE RIVER

The river of your life flowed
from a more distant source than you suspected.
It rises still, a devious flood
between green banks of summer.
It is there forever,
tracing a prophecy across the earth.

Ross Lockridge, Jr., *Raintree County*

DAVE ETTER

Go Read the River

UNIVERSITY OF NEBRASKA PRESS · Lincoln

Thanks are due the following magazines in which many of these poems first appeared: *Antioch Review* (for " But I Loved My Grandma "), *Arbor, Beloit Poetry Journal, Carolina Quarterly* (for "Wedding Day," copyright 1964 by Carolina Quarterly), *Chicago Review, Choice* (Chicago), *December, The Fiddlehead, FOCUS/Midwest* (for "Springfield, Illinois," " The Last Spring of an Old Family Name," "Wind in the Tall Corn," " 4th of July," " Go Read the River," " Notes for Marc Chagall," " On Growing Old in a Quiet Town," copyright 1962, 1963, 1964, 1965 by FOCUS/Midwest Publishing Co. Reprinted by permission), *Genesis West* (for " The Hitchhiker," " Snapshot"), *The Humanist* (for "Summer Sequence," reprinted by permission of the American Humanist Association), *The Husk, Kansas Magazine, Kayak, Mad River Review* (for "Autumn on the Wabash "), *Massachusetts Review* (for " Words for a Friend . . . ," " The Episcopal Windows on John Street," "Two Dreams of Kansas," " In Dubuque County," "The Hometown Hero Comes Home," © 1965 by the Massachusetts Review, Inc. Reprinted by permission), *Michigan's Voices, Midwest, Midwest Quarterly* (for " Homesick in a River Town," " Theme in Yellow," copyright 1964, 1965 by The Midwest Quarterly), *Minnesota Review, New Mexico Quarterly* (for " Sun Dance Sun "), *Omnibus* (for " The Tree Chopper "), *Parallax, Patterns, Poetry Northwest, Prairie Schooner, San Francisco Review, South Dakota Review, Tri-Quarterly,* and *Wormwood Review* (for " As You Travel Ask Us," " The Girlie Magazines," " Twisted Apples ").

To the memory of my aunt

LOUISE GOODENOW

The Noblest and Most Faithful Friend of My Life

CONTENTS

GO READ THE RIVER

I AND THE VILLAGE

I will wear my best green face
and put on a strawberry hat.
Today I will turn this town
upside down and inside out.
I will stop and sing the old songs
at the houses of my townsmen:
yellow houses, lavender houses,
houses with chickens and uncles,
houses with hunchbacks and apples.
Today I will kiss all the farm girls
and play my silver violin
on the marble steps of the courthouse.
And I will tip my strawberry hat
to every green face I see.

THE HOMETOWN HERO COMES HOME

This train, two Illinois counties late,
slips through jungles of corn and hot leaves,
and the blazing helmets of huge barns.

My head spins with too much beer and sun
and the mixed feelings of going home.

The coach window has melted my face.
I itch where a birthmark darkens my skin.

The Jewish woman who sits next to me
sheds tears for a son, dead in Viet Nam.
Her full lips are the color of crushed plums.
I want to go off with her to some lost
fishing village on the Mississippi
and be quiet among stones and small boats.

My fever breaks in the Galena hills.

It's too humid: no one will meet me.
And there are no brass bands in Dubuque.

WEDDING DAY

A blackbird sulks on the window sill
where I have carved a dozen hearts.

I am in love with gin and sleep.

Between the long shadows of red barns
a strange girl calls me to a marriage
under honeysuckle strung with bees.

High in this cupola bedroom
I drift off in a bell of leaves.

Soon, I will never be seen again.

WORDS FOR A FRIEND WHO WAS ACCI-
DENTALLY SHOT WHILE HUNTING
PHEASANTS IN NORTHERN IOWA

. . . a day that has tasted the grief in our blood.
Pablo Neruda

Close weather wets the bricks on Hill Street.
Only one porch light fights the fog.

The midnight train to Mason City
is washed in rivers of the moon.

In the windy cave of a cornfield
your blood has dried on the bones of husks.

I have every right to love you.

INVITATION TO A YOUNG RIVER QUEEN

Purple fish leap for the sun.

The sun is my yellow hat
which I have tossed madly
into the bug-colored air.

I am quite beside myself with joy.

I love the fountains of grass
that spill over the river's edge.
I love worms and stones and bare toes.

You must come fishing with me.

You must come with your raintree sex,
your breasts of Easter eggs,
your thighs of taffy and moonflowers.

And you must wear your yellow hat.

A FIRE OF ROSES

Behind the Victorian house,
a bonfire of cinnamon roses.

Children, quiet as scrapbooks,
wear Halloween masks
and point to the flames.

A trolley car hums through
a tunnel of elm leaves.

Where, where is Miss Maude?

The roses offer a shawl of smoke.

On the grass, a lavender hat.

ILLINOIS PIONEER'S DIARY: AUGUST 12, 1832

(For My Mother)

After my vexing, dull chores were done,
and surrounded by baskets of corn,
I sang under the summer oak trees,
going over and over again
the sad hymns we sing so loud in church.

Then turning to poetry and Burns,
I recited to the frogs and bees,
Pa's favorite, "Man Was Made to Mourn."
The words melted in fevers of sun,
and I was wedded to trees and corn.

TWO DREAMS OF KANSAS

1

Forty-two grain elevators
have blown up
in Salina, Kansas.
I am buried in a loaf
of Sunbeam bread.

2

In a wheatfield
west of Hays,
the fat thighs of a farm girl
are clamped around my loins.
I am dying of loneliness.

TWISTED APPLES
(*After reading Sherwood Anderson's* Winesburg, Ohio)

Even the smashed
scarecrow
flaked out on
the tumbled fence
is not nearly
as grotesque
as these twisted
apples
that redden
the hard ground
What puny
specimens
what ruined flesh
But also
what temptation
to try one
to sink the teeth
down deep
and suck for juice
then spit out
the small seeds
against the rude
and ruthless
weather

WIND IN THE TALL CORN

A madcap wind bends back
the scarecrow's broomstick frame,
stumbles me slap-happy
down the Burlington track.
Strong gusts in the tall corn
set the tassels dancing.
Seven crows come to caw.
A girl with beefy thighs
wipes sweat off her red face,
then disappears in leaves.
Circus wind blows me wild
and woolly toward the house.
Beyond the railroad track
the scarecrow breaks his neck,
cries murder up his sleeve.

DOG DAYS

Back now from
the sand-blasted
city park
where a good
Salvation
Army band
is blowing up
a heat wave
(and Edward
my friend
you knew damn well
they didn't know
"Perdido")
I am belted
by a sharp rain
of dried leaves
(some spin
like tipsy tops)
And among
fuzzy-headed
dandelions
next (shabby) door
where trees are
bare as barns
is a new sign
that demands
FOR SALE
which reminds me
in this grotesque
August weather
how many more
elms can you kill
you Dutch elm
(bastard) beetle?

HEARTS

This you must know:

The pretty girl
with the spring-wind hair,
who has carved hearts
on every single
sycamore tree,
is not in love with you,
is not even in love.
But she found this knife
which has a long,
wicked cutting edge.

You see how it is, boy?

And she must make her mark,
must dig into the sap,
the warm flesh of life,
to touch and cut and shape.

This you must know.

LINES FOR A YOUNG NOVELIST WHO IS ABOUT TO BEGIN ANOTHER WEEK OF WORK AT THE BICYCLE FACTORY

Six o'clock stands tall as a pencil.
Your legs are cramped in the tomb of your bed.

Behind the remains of a circus poster
the diesel trucks snarl like tigers.

Strong words are burning in your belly
and thousands of empty yellow sheets
are floating before the webs of your eyes.

Dry leaves are scratching against the screen.

THE CHILDREN
(For Emily)

Their young need is
to shape red clay soil

and to take such care
so that the breasts

of Pocahontas
(wet with spring rain)

will swell full-mooned
from the dark schoolyard

WHERE I AM

My wife draws a scarlet kangaroo
where once we hung Toulouse-Lautrec.

The baby dreams in her crib of eyes
and runs from Humpty Dumpty.

Beyond the crawling tomato vines
an owl digs my grave on the moon.

4TH OF JULY

Under
a speech
making
at the courthouse
sun
yippee boys
Yankee Doodle
the flag
waving
weather
with their toy
drums
and firecrackers
spoil the games
of little girls
who scoop up
candy
colored
balls & jacks
to run away
in full retreat
flanked by troops
and jeered by
J.
P.
Sousa

BASEBALL SPRING

The home plate was a brick, first base a brick, second base a tin can,
third another tin can.

Carl Sandburg, *Always the Young Strangers*

On the baseball grass
first basemen grow tall,
dream of going 4 for 4
in Yankee Stadium.

Girls in white pinafores
sit on front porch steps
and run cool fingers
over their beautiful calves.

Box-scored fathers mutter
about home runs and daughters,
spill Pabst Blue Ribbon
on their Sunday shoes.

CICADAS

after
a long rain

sun-stung
cicadas

with bright
onion skin

wings
razor

the heavy
yellow air

to wiry
music

and red-eyed
summer

climbs
back to love

twanging
ragtime

PICNIC

And here's the way it was:

An avalanche of thighs
around the picnic table,
chicken wings and cherry pie,
bad jokes and belly laughs;
then sleepwalking rain—
"Get under the elm, the elm,"
screamed Grandma (gulping
her third gin & tonic,
cleverly disguised
as lemonade).
And later Nell and I
turned down watermelon
and volleyball,
and behind the bandstand
played goosey-goosey games.
And the sweat of our sex
was honeysuckle,
was chicken grease.

And that's the way it goes.

Today's last riverboat has come (with cheers) and gone,
and Hannibal, Missouri, settles down again,
sweat-soaked, dog-day groggy in the fierce summer sun.
Dusty roads are almost deserted to pink pigs
that grub and snort among last evening's melon rinds.
Water Street clerks, tired of talk about city girls,
throw away cigars and tilt back splint-bottom chairs
to drowse and dream through their river-lapped reveries.
The town drunkard and a stringbean, fatherless youth,
who is now learning the wayward ways of whiskey,
are fish-deep in sleep on the small stone-fisted wharf;
while beyond the jail and John Clemens' whitewashed fence,
the wild, river-eyed boys tie up their "Injun Joe."

THE POET DREAMS OF HIS YOUTH

The sad music of cello and bassoon.

The corn leaves are yellow.
I can never see them as green.

Sunflowers grow 20 feet tall
and stare the Bible from my eyes.

Hands that have burst their purple veins
float on the river where I was baptized.

In a tree of paper flowers
a calico girl makes Valentines.

Every man, woman, and child of my youth
is standing by his own gravestone.

A boy with a red fish comes toward me at dusk
out of the yellow corn leaves.

The sad music of cello and bassoon.

Over the silent river of dawn
huge fish sail through the blue air.

Houses are sliding into the water
with cargoes of heavy sleepers.

The golden pendulums of old clocks.

Lovers of small yellow apples.
Lovers of lilacs and cinnamon leaves.

A small boat comes through the mist,
and a boy, and a red violin.

AS YOU TRAVEL ASK US

On the left the Saxby home. There are four Saxby boys, all of whom can move their ears.

George Ade, *The Tortures of Touring*

And these kids can
move their asses too,
especially after
letting a car have it
with a few tomatoes.
I've seen them do it.
SPLAT: four ripe ones smack
some old codger's Chevy,
and before Granddad
knows what happened
these rascals vanish
and laugh to beat hell
all the way back home,
where under the elms
they roll around like dogs
gone mad with fleas.

HOLLYHOCKS

Hollyhocks are swaying gently
under the blue branches of an elm.

I watch 82 freight cars
sink into the corn leaves
and drop over the rim of the prairie.

On my back now, I watch the sky
make wool pictures of mothers.

Two blackbirds fly toward the river:
the muddy river of endless regret.

I could lie here forever
and look up at these hollyhocks.

I will never get on in the world.

DROUGHT YEAR

The high-tension wires
string up the western sun.

Near the City Limits sign
(black with bullet holes)
a lean wind fools
in the cottonwoods
and a single cornstalk
rattles its yellow teeth
under the slow drift
of a buzzard's cloud.

Off the sticky blacktop
tumbled gravestones
whisper of burning barns
and the fevered brows
of heatstroked children.

In a weedy creek bed
the whiskey bottle
has a sun devil's eye.

IN DUBUQUE COUNTY
(For Raymond Roseliep)

The mournful horns of diesel trains
enter the farmhouses of Dubuque County.
Also moonlight. Also sounds of corn.

O many an Iowa farmer
is sleeping on the graveyard hill
where cedar trees are grouped like Sisters.

And God walks between the corn rows.
Also gravestones.
Also the farmhouses of Dubuque County.

TWO BEERS IN ARGYLE, WISCONSIN

Birds fly in the broken windows
of the hotel in Argyle.
Their wings are the cobwebs
of abandoned lead mines.

Across the street at Skelly's
the screen door bangs against the bricks
and the card games last all day.

Another beer truck comes to town,
chased by a dog on three legs.

Batman lies drunk in the weeds.

AUTUMN ON THE WABASH

In shadows fishing sycamores
a gold leaf seeds the river.

Red dogs round up the rabbit holes.
(Let me hear that old guitar.)

In a lean sun that saps our days
my brown boat farms the Wabash.

THE HITCHHIKER
(For Dave Herrling)

When trucks and farmers
in Fords won't stop,
and you're famished,
and you know your girl
paces the veranda
of her clapboard house
in Oskaloosa,
there are always rocks
to throw at God,
Elsie the Borden Cow,
and the Green Giant.

Smack 'em real good,
right between the eyes.

That's the way to go.

THE MIDNIGHT FOX

Through fields of ragged corn,
the midnight fox

wears a moon on his back,
but still eludes

on weary legs
the pack of yelping dogs.

Now, the grim-faced hunter
(blister-sore in new boots)

blasts off his shotgun twice.
A corn ear smacks the ground.

The moon turns fox.

FLIGHT PATTERN

The brown paper
airplane
looped once
looped twice
then dove
smack dab into
a flower bed
of four-o'clocks.
The boy was damn tired
of watching only
two little loops
then KERPLUNK,
so butchered
the brown paper
airplane
with his jackknife.
This put a bad crimp
in the big plans
to make Jasper Street
an important
air center.
Later his aunt
said it was
the awful heat
and especially
the strong odor
of four-o'clocks
that did it.

BLACK WAS THE COLOR

(The burning of the Shenandoah Valley, 1864)

This burned out valley coughs fear
in a sweat of birdfall sleep.

Graveyards choked with stone, scorched fields,
fire-flattened barns, charcoaled winds,
shape the sapped and cindered night.

A star-crossed eye of moonlight,
blind as courthouse clock, stares down
dreams in their beanstalk growing.

An old soldier, who rode with Jackson,
whittles sticks into a cobweb of memories
and spits tobacco juice on his wooden leg.

Soft crying: a widow, since Chancellorsville,
buries her grief under the windowpane.

Bleeding now at smoky dawn,
the red sun has a black eye
and a hush of Sunday boils
in the mute and martyred bells.

IN GUTTENBERG, IOWA

In a shady side yard
in Guttenberg, Iowa,
in a white linen suit,
find not Mark Twain
but Big Ed Muehlebach,
who sits there smoking—
an old steamboat pilot dreaming
with his lazy collie dog
by a lacy willow tree,
while a freight train shakes
down to river-sucked Dubuque
under high bluffs turned
to a child's book of color.
Now, Big Ed Muehlebach,
neat in his white linen suit,
watches a towboat push upriver
eight barges filled with coal
(after locking through
Lock and Dam No. 10).
And Big Ed Muehlebach
never thought of Mark Twain
on his long, gull-blown stretch
on the Mississippi.

THE GIRLIE MAGAZINES
(For Rob Cuscaden)

(Ah here they are)

Pink taffy
nipples
top breasts
too creamy
too perfect
there is no
female
who has steep hills
of flesh
like this blonde
Only from
the skilled use
of a brush
and wet dream
of an artist
(too much alone)
could this
nude come forth
to stand here
between pages 12
and 14
of a sex mag

(I'll buy this one)

Tea rose grandmothers
tap-tapping canes down
buggy Water Street,
a tough (stuffed) cougar
next to where Benson's
barber shop once was,
and that crazy Kent kid
blowing in a Coke bottle,
is all I can say when
you ask me: "Hey Dave,
what's been new with you,
and what's blondie's name?"
Oh yes, and licorice sticks
came in at Frampton's Drugs.
Here, have one, Fatty.
Here, have two, Fatty.

FRAGMENTS FROM AN ILLINOIS SCRAPBOOK

1

Drum-taps of rain all night long.

2

In Nauvoo the grapes have been picked
and wine bottles wait in blue cellars.

3

Ghosts of bearded chicken farmers
are kneeling under the Mormon trees.
Their boots are crisscrossed with blood.

4

Clapboard houses in Knox County
contain girls who married Mozart.

5

Men who loved Stevenson and Altgeld
are singing hymns to Jesus
in coal towns south of Effingham.

6

The Rock River moon goes to bed
in the wigwam of a leaf.

7

Drum-taps of rain all night long.

THE LAST SPRING OF AN OLD FAMILY NAME

A cardinal
(half-hidden
in oak leaves)

shakes out his bright
heritage
over this small

family plot
of gravestones
where I stare

at my own
remembered
roll call of names

The cardinal
(his feathers
all slicked down)

flies away
to the green edge
of a cornfield

where I lose him
in the warm
red sunshine

I return now
to muse among
these gravestones

The proud names
bang in my ears
like screen doors

And I am loved
in a hundred
springtime places

A NOSE FOR NEWS

Popcorn
(bacon-
flavored)
scattered
all over
church steps
will remain
there all day
(Monday)
because
around in back
the janitor
(just up from
take-your-time
Alabama)
is beating
out Dixie
on a fake
Persian rug
which when
in place
leads to the
men's room
which is
all out of
paper towels
(and soap)
And I want
to know
is any
of this
church news?

SCHOOLHOUSE

The fat sun of midday
churned our milky brains
to buttermilk
as we laughed and war whooped
through Roy Goodenow's
cornfield
on our way to toss stones
at the abandoned
one-room schoolhouse.

After the first smash
of brittle glass
we drew near to find
the chalky ghost
of old Miss Krause
writing in bat blood
15-letter words
(at least five feet high)
on the dusty blackboard.

Cicadas sang
beyond sycamore trees.
A corn wind blew red dust
in eyes that had blinked
at too much sun.
And when Jack pulled the bell
we all ran away
through Roy Goodenow's
cornfield.

THE TREE CHOPPER

chopped down
a scrawny tree
yesterday

peach
dead
and more fun

I need
a whole forest
to fool in

SNAPSHOT

Noontime
no need for
a flash bulb
and the shot
of an old stone
railroad bridge
in Dixon Illinois
turned out sharp
Marvelous said
the great editor
look for it
in our Fall issue
But the mag
folded

SPRINGFIELD, ILLINOIS

Springfield, Illinois,
has no Altgeld,

no Vachel Lindsay,
no Stevenson.

Springfield, Illinois,
has gone to sleep

under a milktoast sky
near Masters' sweet Sangamon

and Lincoln's brave New Salem.
Only cicadas,

high-strung in elm trees,
reach for the sun

in this torpid town,
and their brief joy

is a sad joy.
Springfield, Illinois,

is a fickle lover,
forgotten.

No more clear-eyed men
come around any more

and her prairie songs
have dead words.

Smoky autumn:
straight shots
of amber sun
pour through
the tangled
park elm trees
where bent
old men sit
to talk about
the railroads
and muse
on that last
amber fourth
of a fifth
of Old Crow
(buried deep
among frayed
shirts across
the IC tracks).
And why can't
Charlie Potts
remember
to bring along
his dad-blamed
hip flask?

THEME IN YELLOW

A cold wind from Waterloo
loosens the yellow apples.

They fall in the side yard and roll
to where an old willow tree
breathes through her thin hair.

The street light moves
on a yellow hair ribbon.

My mother died in a yellow nightgown.

It sweeps the worn kitchen floor
on windy, sleepless nights.

SNOW CONES

Ho for Kansas, land that restores us
When houses choke us, and great books bore us.

Vachel Lindsay

We licked strawberry snow cones
in Wichita, Kansas,

that night by the river.
I remember the humid

June heat and the bent willows,
breathless as we were.

I remember bright moonlight
in Wichita, Kansas,

and how we skipped stones across
the dark Arkansas River.

But, always, always, always,
I'll remember those snow cones,

cold as a Kansas winter,
and how we left them to melt

under a white-thighed moon
beneath the plunging trees.

[45]

MARBLES

Now ten years old,
he carries
a big leather
bag of marbles
down his home block,
slouching with
its rock weight,
to a match game
with the champ
of Maple Street.
And what great hopes
will roll with
that favorite
blue-green agate,
there in the smooth
circle of dirt
by the pear tree.

BICYCLE

Ever since he died
(in a sports car
of a friend's friend)
his old red
bicycle
(that knew a paper route)
has remained propped
against the screened porch
of the clapboard house
to rust with
alternate slants
of sun and rain
And this crab grass end
of Cedar Street
is quiet for once
and the new boy
keeps the evening news
out of the tulip bed
But damn it all
I liked Phil Jones
who rests in peace
at the pine cone end
of Cedar Street
And why doesn't
someone put away
his old red
bicycle?

BUT I LOVED MY GRANDMA

A sweet pea
stuck in each
grass-stained ear
sneaks up barefoot
behind
soapsuds Grandma
with a dead-fly
fly swatter
Swats her topknot
(hard hard hard)
Take that
for not frying
doughnuts
(you promised me)
And that
for not telling
about
Jesse James
And this
for being so
old old old

NUDE

She faces
the spicy sun
from a kneeling
position
her bright head
thrown back
to remove
a blue shadow
that was brushing
her full lips
Her pear-shaped
breasts
hang down
like sun-burst
fruit
and amber
summer grass
rises up
to tickle
the blonde hairs
on her tan
forearms
She poses
with patience
known only
to camels
and Chinese
philosophers
while across
the stony field
two beavers
soak their tails
in creek water

THOREAU: IN SEARCH OF HUCKLEBERRIES

Summer: hillsides of ripe huckleberries
just short minutes from Concord's busy hub.
Bored with Emerson's transcendental talk,
he plucks perfect fruit off a hearty shrub.

Happy he chose this green road not taken,
he squeezes the firm flesh of his desire,
loving the warm purple juice, forsaken
until he stretched forth his cool hand of fire.

OLD DUBUQUE

There is no past, present and future time
here in Dubuque, there is just Dubuque time.

Richard Bissell

From Grant's grave Galena
we drove down in a daze
(from two days of antiques)
to the Mississippi,
then crossed over at noon
to old, hunchbacked Dubuque:
a never-say-die town,
a gray, musty pawnshop,
still doing business; while
on the bluff, blue jeans flap
in a river wind laced
with fresh paint and dead carp.

We couldn't find the house
where she once lived and died
(at ninety, baking bread)
somewhere in the hard maze
of crusty shops and streets.
And Dubuque is a spry,
goofy-sad river gal,
lost in a patchwork haze
of tears and years gone by;
and I love this mad place
like my dead grandmother
loved her steins of Star beer.

SUN DANCE SUN

sun dance sun

Apache brazen
Shoshone bold

war dance sun
war paint bright

assaults the cold

swift sassy
brave brassy

arrows of sun

bleed the day

to a tomahawked
scarlet death

in the crisp
Indian summer

afternoon

GHOSTS OF TRAINS

By the forgotten railroad track
summer weeds grow tall as Lincoln.

We lie here in thick yellow weeds.
We talk: the heat shapes our love words.

Ghosts of trains. Whistles in the night.
Sounds of love, crossed with youth and pain.

Trains bound for Denver, Chicago;
trains we lost in lonely cornfields.

I rest my head on your moist thighs.
Your big breasts coax my passion up.

It is strange we should meet again.
My loins ache. The hot night breathes hard.

FROM A 19TH-CENTURY KANSAS PAINTER'S NOTEBOOK

I always paint pictures
of violent weather
(mostly tornadoes
with thick dragon tails
that strike like snakes),
then give them away
to queasy aunts
and quaking uncles.
Though I find peace
in strawberry sunsets,
and those May wine days
when a clover breeze
ding-dongs the tulips,
I am obsessed
with steep funnel-shaped clouds
and frightened children
who cry and run scared
through towering cornfields.
I paint only
the dark-stained pictures
that storm in my head.

THE OLD RAIL

Again the old rail
(my Uncle Chandler)
brings us lumps of coal
and big brass buttons
in a brakeman's cap.

From the rusty
cemetery of trains
he brings us the M&StL
and the Iowa Central
in a battered caboose.

In a timetable suit
he comes to this town
of silent tracks
and lost spur lines
yelling "highball."

And then he talks of
the Kate Shelley bridge,
Mikado type locomotives,
and mile-long freights
to Eagle Grove.

ROMP

her
strong
white
legs
are
wet
grass
stained
I
help
her
up
she
grabs
my
neck
rubs
cool
milk
weed
in
my
hot
face
and
I
am
glad
she
chose
to
run

SUMMER SEQUENCE

Beyond the barn
sweet red clover
is robbed by bees
with amber knees

Sunflowers
mock the sun
in fields where
rabbits run

A dry-eyed speech
by roadshow dust
chokes up the Ford
now left to rust

At moist noon
sticky June
squeezes out
lemon juice

Old folks rock in
bittersweet shade
shooing the flies
that summer made

MOONFLOWERS

River roads of insects
rub summer in the ears
of slow farmers.

In the sweet crotch
of a sassafras tree
Janet sucks hard candy
and jabs brown toes
at her little brother.

A wind out of Kansas
carries rumors
of wild wheat fires
and the blue eyes
of young soldiers.

Near the screen door
moonflowers bloom:
shy faces of farm girls.

YOKNAPATAWPHA

The first eye had seen the flood;
The second eye had watched Christ die.

Kenneth Patchen, *The Dark Kingdom*

After the worst of the flood,
swelling with cats and dark flowers,
a golden rain barrel was found,
come down from the goodbye river.

(Boys
were sobbing in barns,
bewildered
among oily shotguns and mules,
and a trunk of broken
toys.)

And when the boards were pried loose
by nervous fingers caked with mud,
the mutilated skull of Christ
rolled out into the rotgut sun.

MIDNIGHT AND STILL LATER

(Remembering the Minneapolis & St. Louis Railway)

Endless west-rolling freight trains:
an iron night of bells
(ding-ding-ding-ding-ding-ding)
at the Third Street crossing.

The nervous headlights cut through
the bugged and barking air
to dig up blue flowers
from their weedy graves.

All summer the flowers
are cuffed by wind, fried by sun.
But something proud here wants to live:
one more day, one more week.

A battered M&StL boxcar,
lashed to Chicago & North Westerns,
moves toward Iowa.
It, too, digs up blue memories.

AFTER A LONG NIGHT IN KEOKUK

Morning
(pale as a fish)
slips inside
and rooftops
spin away
to a forest
of burnt corn
and birdsong
shrivels up
the leaves
in the round
Grant Wood trees
We lie here
in bed
in a motel
in Keokuk
Iowa
and we got gin
and we got smokes
and we got your
sad childhood
to talk about
(and mine too)
And I refuse
to answer
the phone
or the knuckles
on our door

NOTES FOR MARC CHAGALL

Under the kissing trees
boys and purple chickens
run through old dandelions
(a world of grandmothers).

The town clock sports a red face
and a mouthful of grapes.

Midnight: tents are being pitched
beyond cornfields and castles.

Restless in warm vineyards,
between black bread houses,
peasant girls with circus thighs
cry in the wings of lilies.

RIVERBOAT SHORE LEAVE

This old county seat town
(caged in a jungle of corn)
contains 13 beer bars
with the usual wide
selection of nuts,
one pigeoned RR station
on the Rock Island Line,
one sweaty-eyed courthouse clock,
and most significant,
one buggy screen door
which I can knock on,
then stagger inside
to a cucumber sandwich
and a bottle of Grain Belt.
And there is always
a fooling around session
with Penelope Jane
(after Uncle Max
takes off for a game of pool
or a round of golf),
which often leads to
a mammoth four-poster bed,
where three people have died
in their damp summer sleep
from too much summer heat.
(And sex was never blamed.)

THE EPISCOPAL WINDOWS ON JOHN STREET

(*For Barbara Whitney*)

Behind grimy sycamore trees,
slowly wintering toward leaf time,

the stained-glass windows of the Episcopal church
turn to silent hymns of burgundy and gold.

Early this morning I walked up John Street.
The cold sun put flames at the windows.

And I heard again my childhood's sober music,
and saw our Sunday faces carved in stone.

SNOW COUNTRY

only
a little
yellow

school bus
creeping along
a thin

ribbon
of snow road
splashed color

on the white
winter canvas
that was

Wyoming
from the train
yesterday

NOTES ON A DRY SEASON

Autumn leaves are piled up high
in all the long gutters.

The wind has red teeth.

Nearby, on Dead Man's Hill,
two oaks brood like jailers.

The tree house sucks on a match.
Towheaded boys scramble
down two-by-four steps
and yell out "fire, water, fire."

I hull black walnuts
and watch leaves turn to dust.

My fingers are dark stained.

RETURN

The shed is leaking seeds and leaves
where once I hid to smoke a pipe.

An apple bloods the rotting floor.

A broken rake with one tooth left
is wrapped in hairy spider's clothes.

The orchard on this clumpy hill
has fallen down upon its knees
and shadows thick with hungry birds
are choking off the nesting sun.

I smash a window with the rake.

Then shine the apple on my sleeve.

PROGRESS REPORT
(*For William Carlos Williams*)

yesterday
they cleaned up

forgotten debris
between dark walls

of the hospital
you wrote about

but never touched
the smooth pieces

of that broken
green bottle

in the hearty sun

THE FORGOTTEN GRAVEYARD

I have left my townsmen down below
under the shadows of Town Hall:
religious fakers, Republicans,
the windbags at the barber shop.

On this hill, the clean smell of skunk.

The ape-faced trees crouch like gnarled bootblacks
over the yellow tombstones;
and there is a bird's nest—a torn blue wig.

But I am at home among the dead,
the deformed, the discolored.

A woodpecker joyfully carves his hole.

The sunset sweetens the mouth of a leaf.

MARCH

At the muscled beach,
stupefied by kites,
old men read the labels
of sardine cans.

The wind builds islands
in the seas of my head
where Norwegian sailors
are calling lost cats.

I close my eyes
and dream of tall ships
and castaway queens
on lonely shores.

COURTHOUSE SATURDAY

As I munch a 10¢ bag of popcorn,
dead leaves collect
under two cannons at the courthouse
where rowdy boys ride
the ugly black guns
into bloody twilights.

Now, a pumpkin-face girl
with enormous boobies
bounces up the stone steps
with legal papers in her chubby hand.
And I am out today to see all I can see:
college students from Thailand,
baton twirlers with shiny knees,
candy suckers, pipe puffers,
fat women with hairy legs
who are in love with Hershey bars,
surreal real estate salesmen,
bearded bartenders carrying Proust,
male Sunday School teachers
flipping through *Rogue* and *Modern Man* . . .

In sneakers, loafers, sandals,
patent leathers, muddy boots,
the restless citizens of my hometown
walk, strut, and run by me
on an old gold Saturday morning
at the county courthouse.

SHORT STOP

Then we stopped
(June sticky)
in Chillicothe
Ohio
to see my
(jelly roll)
girl cousin
whose belly
shakes with fat
townships
of liquid laughter
And after
sweet mountains
of sponge cake
and much beer
we drove off
and I last saw her
blow me a kiss
(one for the road)
from the back porch
on her way
out back with
a big bag
of empties

THE OWL
(For My Father)

The hulking owl,
with a nose like sharp candy
and a swooping widow's peak,
surveys the eerie dusk
from his favorite
tall tamarack tree.
The sulking owl,
with talons like a condor
and a frozen, heart-shaped face,
refuses to wink away
the burnt out end of day
and betrays the cold quiet
of this mountain lake
with a nervous scraping
of his padded shoulders.

SUNDAY IN KANKAKEE COUNTY

Water from the pump,
a rusty trowel:
red geraniums
are well planted
now on both sides
of your gravestone.

The prairie wind,
the leaves of grass,
the forest smell
of these cedar trees:
O how I wish
I had come sooner.

Please forgive me.

Here, let me wash
that birdcrap off
your middle name.

There, that's better.

Louise I love you.

HOMESICK IN A RIVER TOWN

In the valley of the Wapsipinicon,
schoolgirls are picking leaves off old trees,
autumn ambushed in a wagon wheel wood.

I am cold and homesick in this river town.

All morning I sat by the Indian water
and dreamed among weeds and sleeping willows.

Now I wander in the wood of my lost youth
to hear the carrousel laughter of girls.

My eyes want the backyard faces of trees.
My hands ache for familiar touch and feel.

The wind comes up. I am drowning in leaves.

I am spinning away on a dead maple leaf.
I am rolling down the hill of boyhood
to the red brick town I cannot love.

DECEMBER ON THE RIVER

In this overstuffed, bird-in-a-cage room
the chipped keys of the player piano
are plinking out an old scrapbook tune.

I cannot call out its yellowed name.

Below Lock and Dam No. 11
they are dragging the Mississippi River
for the body of a deckhand from Epworth.

Stoned, leathered, and gimcracked with bad art,
our bluff house of blue lights chills my blood.

The player piano grinds to a quick stop.
All the bouncing keys are frozen stiff.

Snow begins to fall on Locust Street.

LOOKING AROUND THE BACKYARD
I THINK OF OUR LOST CAT
(*For Peggy*)

Rain has washed the boards of the tree house.
The wood is smooth and golden in the sunlight.

The lank leaves of the weeping willow
are turning from pale green to pale yellow.

Our orange cat has been gone seven weeks.
He has been a tiger for quite awhile now.

Soft raindrops pad through the leaves again.
The smell of wet wood is a goodbye smell.

Our orange cat has gone away to see the queen.

ON GROWING OLD IN A QUIET TOWN

The old codgers across the street
at the Presbyterian rest home
are sticking seeds on clammy cardboard.

I want to run away to cornfields.

Summer bathrobes are worn loosely,
exposing the worn inner thighs
of men gone fallow behind bricks.

Night knocks in my head of harvests.

Crows fly among the shrunken pine cones.

A HOUSE BY THE TRACKS

Snow falls, stops, starts again.

Santa Fe Wabash Seaboard

The freight train earth cracks in two.

Nickel Plate Nickel Plate

There are curses on the courthouse wind.

B&O L&N

South of town a farmer has been shot
by a hunter with a Jim Beam face.

Illinois Central Illinois Central
(piggyback piggyback)
Great Northern Great Northern
Pennsylvania Rock Island

Cops are burning up the county roads.

Missouri Pacific

The black branches of mulberry trees
are writing my name on the backs of barns.

Union Pacific Norfolk and Western
Burlington Soo Line Burlington

I have hot coffee on the stove
and fresh doughnuts from the A&P.

Milwaukee Road Nickel Plate
North Western Boston and Maine

I have never been so all alone, so

Erie-Lackawanna

THE UNFOUND DOOR

. . . and all the sad and secret flowing of my life.

Thomas Wolfe

Here in falling Kane County
the gold red brown leaves
drift down slowly slowly
like ships boats sinking

The air is blue bright blue

Oceans seas should be this blue

Oceans should have leaves
falling over them falling
in the rusty noons of fall

The gold red brown leaves
leave their old moorings
and drift off to a strange sea
where men are laughing in cornfields

I too am drifting and sinking
in the slow autumn weather
of Kane County Illinois

But I know now I know now
it is first love of this place
I want to hang on to

GO READ THE RIVER

This little red brick
town by the river

never did see
its prettiest girls

run around naked
in hollyhock yards,

or hear a band
that could play good Dixie.

But that sure isn't why
the place went to pot,

why the sun-bleached shades
are all drawn on Elm Street,

or why the slowest trains
thunder by now

to blow thick dust
against the beer signs.

PRAIRIE SUMMER
(*For Carl Sandburg*)

1

Hollyhocks are blooming in schoolyards
of towns along the Soo Line.

In chicory lots Chevrolets rust
under the Clabber Girl signs.

In Winneshiek County, Iowa,
near where Hamlin Garland once lived,
a whole Norwegian family
is out planting apple trees.

2

Our village of rambler roses
contains cats in trellised shade,
children asleep on islands of moss,
and quiet men who smoke pipes and sit
on stone benches at the courthouse.

3

Heart-shaped leaves fall in the pitcher
of lemonade: 3¢ a glass, 3¢ a glass.

4

Dripping with a sticky green sweat,
my brother, who would be farmer,
walks the highway to Plato Center.

The endless cornfields swell above him.
Heat waves jump up from the concrete.

To breathe deeply is to half drown.

5

The barber's son brings me a gift:
13 butterflies in a cellophane bag.

The grass shudders in the lawnmower.

A bluejay screams in the jaws of the sky.

6

Under the oak tree by the back fence
my beautiful blonde sister
is writing a poem about Altgeld.

Dinner pails are in it. And picks and shovels.
Slow footsteps on broken stairs are in it.
And angry men with Polish names.
Darrow is in it. And Debs and Sandburg.

Next week she will read it aloud
to the Women's Club and the DAR.

7

Below a bluff of yellow tombstones
two houseboats gather old shadows
and the waves of a speedboat.

Time for bare feet, beer, and box scores.

8

What do sunflowers talk about after dusk
when the wind goes down and the moon comes up?

9

I love to sit here on the screened porch
and go over the names of prairie towns:
Morning Sun, Carbon Cliff, What Cheer;
and the Indian names of rivers:
Wapsipinicon, Kishwaukee, Pecatonica.

10

After the band concert in the firefly park
katydids sing above a circus of weeds—
weeds that are hiding a whiskey bottle,
a new baseball, and a book of magic.

11

Midnight: rain beats on the clapboards,
soaks the grass, cleans the walks.

Wonderful, the smell of tomato vines.

Far off, the lusty wail of diesel horns:
beef to Chicago, tractors to Omaha.

12

Tomorrow, bumbling among bees,
I will be fisherman,
seeker of lost railroads,
and ambassador to all the forgotten
kingdoms of Chautauquas and streetcars.

POETRY

Go Read the River is the first collection of poems by Dave Etter, whose work has previously appeared in some fifty magazines, among them *Antioch Review, Beloit Poetry Journal, Chicago Review, Choice, Massachusetts Review, Prairie Schooner,* and *New Mexico Quarterly.* Mr. Etter, who is Assistant Editor of Encyclopaedia Britannica, was born in California in 1928, went to the University of Iowa (B.A. in history, 1953), and now lives in Geneva, Illinois. He has this to say about his poetry:

> I am obsessed with the American Middle West and most of my poems are the result of that obsession.

> I write only about what deeply interests me: rivers, cornfields, railroads, courthouses, graveyards, for instance. And always people interest me most.

> I write free verse, rhythmically controlled; free rhythms strongly influenced by jazz and folk songs. Images abound; I love to use color as much as possible.

> My images are dredged out of the Middle Western landscape. I am a poet who prefers to take his materials from the little prairie towns and farm country; I have a deep dislike of cities and industrialization.

> My themes run from great joy to deep sadness; loss is a principal theme. There is also anger and (I hope) humor too. There is nostalgia for the past; but also an attempt to feel at home in the modern world. I am somewhat pessimistic about the future, however.

Cover design by Jerry Graff